Writer to Writer: How to Conference Young Authors

The Bill Harp Professional Teacher's Library

Writer to Writer: How to Conference Young Authors

Tommy Thomason

Texas Christian University

Christopher-Gordon Publishers, Inc.
Norwood, MA

Credits

Every effort has been made to contact copyright holders for permission to reproduce borrowed material where necessary. We apologize for any oversights and would be happy to rectify them in future printings.

Conference Checklist from *And With a Light Touch: Learning About Reading, Writing, and Teaching with First Graders,* by Carol Avery, used by permission of Heinemann.

Christopher-Gordon Publishers, Inc.
1502 Providence Highway, Suite #12
Norwood, MA 02062
(800) 934-8322

Printed in the United States of America

10 9 8 7 6 5 4 3 2 1   01 02 01 00 99 98

ISBN: 0-926842-79-X

Contents

Foreword

By *Gloria Houston*

I have taught many subjects over a span of many years, and I have come to the conclusion that certain skills and sets of skills cannot be taught; they can only be learned. In those situations, the teacher does not teach. The teacher can act only as guide, mentor, and coach.

Performing as a musician involves sets of skills that may be learned through repetition, practice, and refinement. A music teacher plays many roles in the learning of those skills. In fact, in music vocabulary, a teacher is always called a *coach*. He demonstrates technique, coaches, mentors, guides, and encourages until the student reaches the point of refinement at which she goes beyond playing notation and begins to play music. I spent most of my early life as a music teacher. I know the situation well.

My friends who are athletes or who coach sports tell me that their roles are very similar. As the world's greatest klutz, I have no knowledge of that world. I believe Tommy Thomason when he writes that the roles are similar.

I taught myself to write by writing teaching materials for my elementary music classes—a field in which written materials were usually too complex and convoluted—trying them out on my students, having them give me feedback, and revising them. Even with that experience, I had the impression that a person went to school, was taught to write, and became a writer. So after I was published, I took a writing course, terrified that my audience might learn that I had never been taught to write.

But a funny thing happened in that writing class. I found out that I had learned to write the only way we can learn that set of skills—by writing. I also found out that I had learned many of the skills of writing years before, sitting in my practice room at the piano. My music teachers had been my coaches, and the skills I acquired under their guidance transferred readily to my writing. Practice is nothing more than revision. Practice takes time. Writing takes enormous amounts of practice.

Later, when I began to write with some purpose, my music students were my coaches; their feedback helped me shape and refine both my thinking and my writing and when I wrote my first book, my editor coached and guided me. So, there was no reason for me to be terrified after all. I had learned to write in the only way we can learn to write.

Now when I teach the techniques of teaching writing, my students are always startled to hear me say that it may be that writing cannot be taught, that it may be that it can only be learned. By the end of the semester, most of them agree with me.

I believe that teaching writing consists mainly of the teacher playing the role of coach—demonstrating techniques, guiding practice, mentoring, and encouraging until the writer has refined the piece of written discourse to suit his purpose and audience. The writing teacher is the coach, not the teacher. The traditional skills used by teachers to *instruct* their students simply do not work in guiding young writers to learn to write. Training in sports or music is probably far more valuable.

When guiding novice musicians—or novice writers—the constant feedback so necessary for refinement is provided through *conferencing*: The coach and the player/writer exchange ideas, provide feedback to one another, and refine techniques through practice. In other fields, the term *conferencing* is not used, but whatever it's called, time spent talking with the novice is perhaps the most valuable contribution to the refinement of the piece, whether it is written in words or in musical notation.

This book won't provide a detailed script for your conferencing. What it does is more valuable: It describes the process, supplies lots of motivation, and tells you how you can take conferencing back to your classroom.

That's the reason I was so excited to read this manuscript. It emphasizes the role of conferencing in the learning of writing skills, and it provides carefully organized guidance for the teacher who has been trained in instruction, not coaching. It succeeds in helping the teacher to become a coach, a mentor, and a guide. It is a book I will use in my writing class.

The Awakening

By *Brod Bagert*

I held in my hand a new poem,
Four lines of black-ink adolescence
Scribbled on blue-lined paper,
And as I handed it to my seventh grade teacher,
I drew in my breath,
And watched her lips as she read:

Dragon Song

Green slime, craven, dragon's haven,

Mad dog howls the angel's song!

Beauty dies in a world of lies,

And right is crushed by wrong.

That was thirty years ago,
And now,
As I read my own words,
I find myself tempted to laugh.
But *she* didn't laugh.

"Oh Brod!" she said,
"*You* have an ear for language.
Listen to the sound of your poetry."
And again I held my breath
As she read my words out loud.

It was the simplest of moments,
And yet ... the sound of her voice,
As it passed between us,
Was the harbinger of fate,
A whisper to awaken
The courage to create.

© Brod Bagert 1997

INTRODUCTION

An "Operating Manual" for the Writing Conference

Writing conferences are one of the most talked about and least practiced strategies in the writing process classroom.

Thousands of teachers have attended workshops where conferencing was explained. They left with pages of notes and an earnest desire to conference young writers, but somehow it just didn't work as well as the workshop speaker said it would.

So the writing conference joins the list of "Been There, Done That, Didn't Work" strategies all teachers file away in their minds.

If you would like to dust off that file and reexamine conferencing, this book is for you. Perhaps the reason it didn't work is that conferencing (the term I prefer—*conferring* sounds like something you do in a Senate subcommittee, not a classroom) is a skill. Like writing.

You learn to write by writing, ideally under the mentorship of someone who helps you think through the process and offers valuable advice. That's the same way you learn to conference writers.

This book is written for the busy teacher. No chapter will take longer than five to ten minutes to read. Each chapter introduces a different facet of the writing conference or the philosophy and classroom practice that undergird it. Each chapter ends with a *Something to think about* section to help you implement the ideas you have just read about. When you have finished the book's 14 chapters, you'll be ready to use the ideas for record-keeping in conferences found in the appendix written by veteran first-grade teacher Lois Davila. In the appendix, Lois shares ideas for keeping running records that will save you lots of time and help your conferencing to run more smoothly.

Think of this book as you would the operating manual of your computer. When you got your computer, you probably didn't sit down and read the manual straight through. You read it section by section, completing the hookups or software installation as you went along. By the time you finished, your computer was up and running.

Try reading this book the same way. Set aside 15 minutes a day to read a chapter and work on the *Something to think about* section. By the time you finish the book, the writing conference should be up and running in your classroom writing community.

CHAPTER 1

Talking Writing in Writing Workshop

When Gina Holland, a Detroit-area second grade teacher, listens to the sounds of writing workshop in her class, she can't help but remember her own days as a writer in elementary school.

Those were the days when silence reigned supreme in the writing classroom. Children sat in orderly rows, writing to the prompts their teacher assigned. They completed their assignments, turned them in, and awaited the inevitable red pencil of the teacher. The next day their writing assignments were returned—edited, of course—followed by admonitions to pay attention to the corrections, followed by another writing assignment.

Gina's teacher would be shocked to see Gina's classroom. Gina herself is one of the writers, working alongside the children during the first part of the workshop. Some children sit at tables, some lie on the floor, two nestle down into beanbags, and one sits in a rocking chair in the reading center. As if in a reverie, Gina listens to the sounds of pencils scratching on paper and markers coloring in the final touches on illustrations. Two children, collaborating as author and illustrator on a book about dinosaurs, quietly discuss ways to make a Tyrannosaurus look more ferocious.

But Gina doesn't stay lost in her reverie for long; she knows this is crucial teaching time. Gina always writes with her class so she can demonstrate how to choose a topic, write a lead, and select the information to include in her piece. But after 10 minutes or so of writing, Gina puts her own piece aside to *talk writing* with her class. Talking writing is called a writing conference—a one-on-one conversation between two writers about a work in progress.

As Gina walks around the room, she notices Sergio chewing on his eraser, staring at his almost-finished piece, obviously deep in thought.

"How's it coming?" she asks.

"I think I'm through," Sergio says, "but maybe I need to put more in it."

"What are you writing about?"

"My trip to the zoo. Wanna read it?"

"I'd love to. But why don't you read it to me? I want to hear it in the author's own language."

Sergio reads:

> On saturday, I woke up early. I went to the zoo with my aunt. I saw a tiger. He was walking back and forth in his cage. We had a hot dog at the zoo and then I came home and went to bed. The end.

"I think I've seen that tiger," Gina tells Sergio. "He was pacing back and forth when I was at the zoo, too. What did he look like?"

"He was sort of orange with black stripes that went around his whole body. You could see every muscle in his legs when he walked. He paced [Sergio picked up the word Gina had just used] back and forth like the cage was making him nervous and he just wanted to be free to run in the jungle. I felt real sorry for him."

"Wow!" Gina said. "I loved the way you described the tiger. Can I get some of that down on paper?"

Sergio nodded yes as Gina reached for an extra sheet of paper on his desk.

"You said you could see every muscle in his legs when he walked," Gina said as she wrote. "And then what, about his being nervous?"

Sergio restated his sentence about the tiger who longed to run free in the jungle, adding a few ideas in the retelling.

"That's really good writing," Gina said. "Do you know why?"

Sergio shook his head in the negative.

"Because good writing helps readers picture things in their minds. Close your eyes, Sergio, and listen, while I read you what you just wrote."

Sergio shut his eyes tightly as his teacher began to read:

"I could see every muscle in the tiger's legs as he paced back and forth in the cage. He looked nervous, and I wondered if he was wanting to go back to Africa, where he could run free in the jungle."

A smile spread across Sergio's face as he realized he had just produced a piece of well-written prose.

"Would you like to put that in your story?" his teacher asked.

Strangely, Sergio hesitated. But Gina could read the mind of any second-grade writer.

"If you didn't have to recopy this, would you like it in your story?"
Now Sergio nodded enthusiastically.

"A professional writer would never recopy something like this to add it to the story," Gina said. "If you put it in your piece, where would it go?"

Sergio pointed immediately to the logical place.

"You mind if I take these scissors and cut your piece right where you just pointed?" Gina asked. Sergio said he didn't.

So she cut Sergio's story into two pieces, with the break coming at the place where he said he would insert the description of the pacing tiger. Then she put a #1 on the top of the paper, a #2 on the paragraph he had dictated to her, and a #3 on the last few sentences he had originally written. Then she reached for a stapler to fasten the three together.

"Why don't you share this with Kyle?" Gina said. "You know how much he loves animals."

End of conference. The whole conversation had taken just under five minutes. Later that day, Sergio shared his piece with Kyle, who asked some more questions about the tiger. Those questions led to more revisions in the days following, along with some research in a zoo animal atlas in the classroom. Sergio even discovered that tigers live in Asia, not Africa. The book he published a week later bore little resemblance to the original story he read to his teacher.

The writing conference is one of the most valuable teaching strategies in the process-oriented classroom, because it helps the writer to think through the piece at hand. The writing conference is not meant to create a dependency. Its goal is to help young writers think about the issues any writer must consider during writing. Writing conferences help writers focus on what they have written and talk through ways the writing can be improved.

Something to think about

Think back on your experiences as a writer. Did anyone ever sit down with you, one-on-one, to discuss something that you had written—not to evaluate or edit the piece, but to help you think more clearly about it?

The best way to start a conferencing program is to let your students conference you. Take something you have written and share it with your class. Ask them what they would like to know more about. Get their suggestions about how you could add descriptive detail or dialogue to make your piece better. Then rework that section and show them how you applied their ideas.

Writing conferences are most effective in a community of writers where all are willing to share their words and their works in progress. Be sure to model this process for your students many times over before you conference them.

CHAPTER 2

Coach or Editor: What's Your Approach to Teaching Writing?

Josh clutched his crumpled paper tightly in one hand as he unloaded his backpack into his desk with the other. He couldn't wait to share what he had written with Mrs. Collins.

Josh's family had just returned from a weekend in San Antonio, and a sidewalk guitar player had made a special impression on the fourth grader, who harbored a secret desire to take guitar lessons—a desire he hadn't yet shared with his parents. Josh's father had given him several dollars, which he used to tip the guitarist after the musician played the tunes he requested. On Sunday night, Josh sat at his desk in his room and wrote about the guitar player. Josh had pictured the guitarist in his head and tried to describe him and his music as best as he could.

"Mrs. Collins, we went to San Antonio this weekend and I heard this guy play guitar on the street and he knew every song I asked him to play and I gave him three whole dollars," Josh said without taking a breath. "I wrote about him. Would you like to read it?"

His teacher smiled, pleased that Josh would write something he hadn't been assigned and then share it with her.

"Of course, Joshua, I'd love to read your story," she said, taking it from his hands and settling back into her chair. She mentally noted his use of description as he talked about the guitar player and the way he stayed on the topic of the musician and his music.

She finished, then put the paper down on her desk.

"Joshua, this is a very nice piece of writing," she said. "But you used the word *guitar* throughout, and you didn't spell it correctly. You also left out several commas, and you might want to think about making your lead a little more exciting than 'Our family went to San Antonio last weekend.' But other than that, you did a fantastic job. Why don't you work some on the rewrite today and maybe you can share this with the class."

Mrs. Collins thought she had given Josh a compliment.

But obviously, Josh didn't see it that way. He mumbled a thank-you to Mrs. Collins and took the paper back to his seat, where he crumpled it up and shoved it under the desk.

On Tuesday, Mrs. Collins asked him how the rewrite was coming.

"I lost my paper," he lied.

Mrs. Collins is one of thousands of sincere writing teachers who see their function basically as an editor. These teacher-editors believe that people learn to write by writing and then having a well-meaning teacher point out their mistakes.

In other words, it's the job of a teacher to show students what they have done wrong. Otherwise, how can they ever get it right?

A teacher-editor fills the same basic function as a copyeditor at a newspaper or magazine. Copyeditors work with raw copy. It is their job to make it better—their function is to find errors in grammar and spelling and punctuation and usage, and to fix them. Good copyeditors spot factual inaccuracies, and they fix them. They find places where the writer has lapsed into cliches or redundancy, and they fix them.

Give a good copyeditor a piece of bad copy, and you'll get it back within a few minutes—fixed. No wonder they are prized by their publications.

And no wonder it's so easy to fall into the trap of confusing good editing with good teaching. But there's one crucial difference: *The job of the editor is to improve the **writing**; the job of the teacher is to improve the **writer**.*

When Mrs. Collins read Josh's piece about the guitarist, her initial reaction was that of an editor. She believed, as teacher-editors do, that her role in this situation was to show Josh how he could improve his writing by showing him his mistakes. She acknowledged that he had written a good piece; *fixing* the mistakes would make it even better.

Teachers who see themselves as coaches take a different approach. They sacrifice the editor's short-term goal of clean copy in favor of a long-term goal of improved writers. Coaches realize several important facts about writers of any age:

- Writing is important only when it is personally meaningful. And it is meaningful only when it is seen by the writer as communication with an audience—not as an opportunity for a teacher to give a grade or teach another curriculum objective.

- Writers develop best in a climate that encourages risk-taking and honors initiative. That encourages more writing. And only writing itself—not study *about* writing—develops young writers.

- Writing is more learned than taught. Teachers can demonstrate how they would have done it and give suggestions on how it might be done, but that does more to demonstrate the teacher's expertise than to develop the expertise of the student. Teacher-editors take control of the writing and tell students what do to. Coaches let the writer keep control of the story. They use the writing conference to listen and ask questions and encourage the writer to think about basic writing issues. Coaches believe you improve the writing by improving the writer.

So it is the writing coach who will ultimately adopt the conferencing strategy and use it successfully. Conferencing fits the coaching philosophy because coaches see their job as interacting with writers and their function as getting writers to think about what they have written.

Mrs. Collins was sincere in her desire to improve Josh's writing. But Josh didn't write his piece about the guitarist to develop his writing skills. He had a fourth grader's enthusiasm about sharing on paper something that had made an impression on him. And for all her good intentions, Mrs. Collins effectively told Josh, "I don't care what you have to say; I only care about how you spelled the words and placed the commas."

She couldn't stop being a teacher-editor long enough to listen to what a young writer had to say.

Something to think about

Think about your writing teachers. Did you have any coaches? And what about you? Are you an editor or a coach? Do you focus on the writing or the writer? Do you uphold convention or inspire experimentation? Do you identify weaknesses or build on strengths?

Mark where you are on the editor-coach continuum. Wherever you are, make a list of ways you could function more as a coach in your classroom. Then write a short paragraph telling what difference it would make in your teaching if you worked more as a coach this week.

Where are you on the editor-coach continuum?

Editor   Coach

CHAPTER 3

Writing Conferences as Conversations Between Writers

You've probably taken the pop psychology tests in the Sunday magazine section of your newspaper, tests that determine in just a few short questions how good a lover you are, or how honest you are, or how effective you are as a parent. Here's a simple test that's a much more reliable indicator of your potential to become a great writing teacher.

		Yes	No
1.	Is writing a positive experience for you personally?	☐	☐
2.	Do you consider yourself a writer?	☐	☐
3.	Do you keep a journal, a writer's notebook, or otherwise write on a regular basis?	☐	☐
4.	Do you write regularly with your class during writer's workshop?	☐	☐
5.	Do you share your first drafts with your class?	☐	☐
6.	Do you let your class see your revision and editing process?	☐	☐

If you answered *yes* to at least 4 of those questions, you are probably already a successful writing teacher.

But some teachers wonder, "Can't I teach writing successfully without being a writer myself or if I don't enjoy writing? I'm not a writer, but I know a lot *about* writing."

Schools would never think of assigning a teacher who couldn't drive to teach driver's education. And there's no such thing as a swimming coach who can't swim. Or a band director who can't play a musical instrument. Or a Spanish teacher who can't speak the language.

But American schools have thousands of writing teachers—you may be one—who don't like to write, and don't see themselves as writers, and never write with or for their students.

Some of these teachers go from seminar to seminar on weekends and during the summers, looking for the key that will unlock the door to success in their writing classrooms. Some are even experts on the strategies associated with the process-oriented writing classroom. But something's missing. They're attacking the problem at the wrong end. These teachers are looking for the hidden strategy or approach that will turn their students on to writing. The answer, however, isn't in a strategy. It's in the teacher.

Here's why. Strategies and methods are ultimately outgrowths of the teacher's attitudes toward writing. Your attitudes reflect your philosophy of writing. Many teachers claim they don't really have a philosophy of writing. But they do—they just don't know it.

Your philosophy of writing includes everything you believe about the value and rewards of writing. It includes what you believe about how people learn to write. It reflects how you feel toward writing at the very deepest levels of your being. This philosophy of writing determines your attitudes toward writing, and your attitudes will ultimately determine your instructional strategies.

So what determines your philosophy of writing?

Your philosophy of writing is an outgrowth of your personal experience as a writer. This means your own life as a writer is ultimately reflected in your classroom. So if you want to change your classroom, you have to begin by changing you.

If you don't enjoy writing or don't see yourself as a writer, that's a tall order. But there's good news: It works the same way for teachers as it does for kids. You learn to write by writing. You don't learn to write by studying writing, or going to writing seminars, or preparing to write, or working on your grammar or vocabulary. All those things are important, and all can be useful. But they are the results of writing, not the motivators of writing. Once you are writing on a regular basis, begin to read books on writing or go to a weekend seminar. You'll really benefit from the extra input, and you'll see its effects in your prose or poetry.

But don't keep waiting for that "just right" seminar or book or experience to get your started. It'll never come.

How often have you passed a runner as you drove to school and noticed his or her muscled body and flat stomach and wished to yourself, "I wish I had that runner's desire to run. If I did, I'd run every day." But that thought betrays a faulty assumption—that the runner was motivated to run and therefore started running. First the motivation, then the result.

If you actually stopped your car to talk with the runner, however, you would probably discover that you have it backward. The runner probably started running because he or she knew about the health benefits, then used sheer will power to keep going when the weather was cold or the motivation just wasn't there. The motivation grew out of a running lifestyle. Now the runner is motivated, but the motivation was the result of the running, not the cause of it.

Natalie Goldberg (1986), who is both a writer and a runner, put it this way:

> Some days you don't want to run and you resist every step of the three miles, but you do it anyway. You practice whether you want to or not. You don't wait around for inspiration or the deep desire to run. It'll never happen, especially if you are out of shape and have been avoiding it. But if you run regularly, you train your mind to cut through or ignore the resistance. You just do it. And in the middle of the run, you love it. When you come to the end, you never want to stop. And you stop, hungry for the next time.
>
> That's how writing is, too. Once you're deep into it, you wonder what took you so long to finally settle down at the desk. Through practice you actually do get better.
>
> You learn to trust your deep self more and not give in to your voice that wants to avoid writing. (p. 11)

So how do you begin the writer's journey?

- **Start writing regularly.**   You might begin with, say, 10 minutes a day for four or five days a week. Start your own writer's notebook. That's not a journal, although some days what you write might look a lot like a typical journal entry. A writer's notebook is a place to play with genres, styles, and techniques. Here are some suggestions to get you started:

    √ Begin the picture book you've always wanted to write. Work on it for 10 minutes, then put it down and work on it some more the next day. (By the way, you don't have to finish this or any other writing assignment you give yourself. The object is to write for 10 minutes a day, not to complete any particular project. So if you work for four consecutive days on your picture book and then decide you don't want to write it after all but would prefer to write some poems for your class, don't feel guilty about not finishing. You've accomplished what you set out to do—to write.)

√ Write about your childhood memories or your family or the school you attended as a child. Use dialogue and description.

√ Write letters to the editors of newspapers, magazines, or professional journals. Continue to work on them until you are satisfied, then send them off for possible publication.

√ Write letters to parents of your students explaining your classroom activities, your teaching philosophy, or your plans for upcoming thematic studies.

√ Experiment with poetry. Get out your college English textbook and take a shot at writing a sonnet. Or try haiku or limericks or free verse.

√ Work on description. Find a well-written descriptive passage and just copy it in your writer's notebook. The next day, explain in your writer's notebook why that passage was so well-written. What exactly did the author do that made the piece come alive and cause you to choose that section to copy? Then, on the following day, try your own hand at description. Use the principles you just wrote about the day before to paint a word picture of a person or place or feeling for a reader.

• **Start writing with your class.**   Take at least a portion of almost every writing workshop to write. Try writing on overhead transparencies so you can share your processes and products with your class. Let your class see your false starts and crossed-out sentences—that's how young writers really learn about the writing process. Nancie Atwell (1987) writes about how her modeling of writing affects her young writers:

> I sit down at an empty student desk—so kids can clearly see what I'm doing—with my favorite white paper and favorite Flair pen. I label my manuscript DRAFT #1, put my head down, and start writing one of the stories I'd considered in the minilesson. I don't look up. I'm not watching to see who's writing and who isn't. I'm busy, and I mean business, and my posture demonstrates that I'm expecting everyone else will become a writer and join me.
>
> And they do. After ten minutes or so, when I finally look up from my own writing, everyone is writing. (p. 84)

At this point, you may be asking what all this has to do with conferencing young writers. The title of the book is *Writer to Writer*. Ask any writing coach who successfully employs conferencing as a strategy, and he or she will tell you that the coach must also be a writer. Coaches *earn* the right to conference by sharing their writing processes and products. And the best insights into writing are the insights of a writer—someone who has experienced the joys and despairs of the writing life.

Something to think about

Look back over the two suggestions given at the end of this chapter: starting a writer's notebook and writing with your class. You'll never be more motivated to start these two projects than you are right now. Remember, some teachers say, "I don't write because I can't write well. If I could write better, I would write more." That's logical, but only to nonwriters. A writer would say, "If I write more, I will write better." When you get your writer's notebook, you might begin the first day by writing about how you feel about the act of writing.

References

Atwell, N. (1987). *In the middle*. Portsmouth, NH: Heinemann.
Goldberg, N. (1986). *Writing down the bones*. Boston: Shambhala

CHAPTER 4

Learning to Talk Writing

Imagine yourself at a football game. Everyone around you is a football fan. They follow their team in the sports pages and wouldn't miss a home game; some have played football. The conversation is lively, informed, and free-flowing.

Now assume you are at the same football game, but the people around you don't know a first down from a linebacker. Nobody has ever played the game, and few have even seen a football game. Try to start a conversation. But if the football talk doesn't flow freely, don't blame the game. The people you're talking to just don't know how to talk football.

Or try to start a conversation about writing with anyone—child or adult—who doesn't normally talk about writing. The results will be much the same as your attempted football conversation with someone who isn't accustomed to talking about the game.

How important is it to learn to talk writing? Let's say you're a veteran driver, but you don't know much about how an engine operates. Your engine is making a funny noise, so you take your car to a mechanic. You drive in behind another customer, and you wait while he explains what's wrong with his car. You listen as he talks with the mechanic:

"I think something's wrong with the powertrain. The transaxle doesn't seem to be engaging the transmission or the differential."

Then the mechanic turns to your problem.

"It's making a funny noise," you say.

"What kind of noise?"

"Sort of like ka-pokita, ka-pokita, ka-pokita."

At that point, you wish you understood the basics of the internal combustion engine and had the language to speak intelligently with the mechanic.

When teachers and students have the language to talk about writing, when they are accustomed to talking about what makes writing work, conferences take on both a new vocabulary and a new tone.

Hal Goldman, a fourth grade teacher in Miami, Florida, noticed that Mauna had her hand up as he circulated through his classroom during writing workshop.

"How's your piece coming—are you still working on the one about your trip to the dentist?"

"I'm really stuck, Mr. Goldman."

"So what's the matter?"

"It's this part here, where I'm talking about the dentist filling my cavity. It doesn't seem real, because I don't have enough details to help the reader picture it."

"Oh?"

"Yeah, the first part's okay, where I tell how nervous I was, 'cause I was just telling how I felt. And the last part's okay, where I tell how happy I was because it didn't hurt that much. But the part in the middle—that's the part where he gave me the gas to work on me, and I don't remember enough to be able to explain exactly what he did then."

"You're really thinking like a writer, Mauna. Writers have to describe a situation or an event to really make it come alive for the reader. And if you can't remember it, it's hard to describe. I'll tell you what: Do you know Ms. Henderson, who teaches sixth grade? Her husband is a dentist. If you will remind me at lunch, I'll take you up and introduce you to her. Maybe she can ask her husband to tell her the steps in filling a tooth, and then she can tell you tomorrow. Then you'll have the information to really make this come alive for your readers."

"Wow! That would be great. Thanks, Mr. Goldman."

Hal Goldman's students had the language to talk about writing. He would frequently take passages from books they knew well and ask the question, "Now what makes that such good writing?"

One day Hal shared Gloria Houston's (1992) book *But No Candy*. It is the story of a little girl who loved chocolate candy, who suddenly found that no candy was available during World War II because sugar was being rationed. The book tells how much she enjoyed eating Hershey bars before the war began:

> If the weather was nice, before she ate her candy bar, Lee would climb to her secret place high in the hickory tree Daddy had planted in the sideyard. When she was safely wedged in where the branches of the tree formed a seat, Lee took the Hershey bar out of her pocket. First, she sniffed the chocolate through the brown and silver paper.

Nothing else in the world ever smelled so good. Then she slowly took off the wrapper and smoothed it out on her knees. Finally she unfolded the white paper and ate the little squares one at a time, letting the chocolate melt on her tongue. To Lee, the taste of that chocolate bar was the best thing in the world. (p. 6)

Hal reread that page for his fourth graders and asked, "Now why is that good writing?"

The students were full of insights on the power of descriptive writing. Hal distributed copies of the paragraph for them and they underlined words and phrases that made the passage come alive. He even brought Hershey bars to class and gave each child a piece. The children reread Gloria Houston's description, then closed their eyes and concentrated on the taste of the chocolate, just like Lee had.

Then Hal produced a sack of oranges from under his desk. The class brainstormed what they remembered about the taste of oranges. Then Hal cut the oranges and gave each student a section. The discussion about Lee had sensitized them to a writer's perspective. They didn't eat like fourth graders—they ate like writers. And then, of course, they wrote about the taste of the oranges.

So was it any wonder that Mauna asked the question she did? Or that she was thinking about those kinds of issues?

Writing conferences are most effective when they occur in a classroom where "writing talk" permeates the atmosphere.

Something to think about

As a teacher, you probably enjoy reading and writing. But are you comfortable talking about writing? That is, talking about the techniques of writing and the qualities that make writing effective?

If not, try this. Write down the 15 books your class typically loves the most. That list may include picture books like <u>Brown Bear, Brown Bear</u> or chapter books like <u>Maniac McGhee.</u> Then, in your writer's notebook, write each title at the top of a separate page. For each book, answer this question: "Why is that book so good? " Tell specifically the qualities that convince you that this is a well-written book. Then next week during conference time, look for those same qualities in your students' writing. You'll find yourself saying, "You know, Kaitlyn, your use of dialogue here reminds me of what Bill Martin Jr. did in <u>Ghost-Eye Tree.</u> Whatever made you decide to tell this in conversation—in dialogue—instead of just telling me the story in your own words? That's a characteristic of really mature writing, you know."

Reference

Houston, G. (1992). *But no candy.* New York: Philomel Books.

CHAPTER 5

What Happens When We Conference?

Every child is unique. So is every class and every writing conference. But there are some common threads in all successful writing conferences, whether they occur in first grade or in sixth, in the suburbs or the inner city, with experienced writers or beginners.

Rob was a new teacher who had read about writing conferencing as an undergraduate. He devoured the chapters on conferencing in books by Donald Graves, Donald Murray, and Lucy Calkins, but he knew he needed to observe conferencing firsthand. He was delighted to discover during his first week as a third-grade teacher that one of his colleagues just down the hall in fourth grade was known for her ability to conduct writing conferences with her students.

Rob arranged to visit her class twice during writing workshop. He observed as she moved easily from writing with her students to conducting short conferences with them as they wrote. On the second day he visited, he listened as she conducted longer conferences with children who had signed up to talk with her because they were preparing manuscripts for publication.

Rob was grateful that he had finally seen conferencing in operation. But he also was discouraged because he realized that the fourth-grade teacher's conferencing approach was an outgrowth of her own personality and style. It just wasn't *him*.

Rob called one of his professors to share his frustration.

"Rob, no two writing conferences are alike," Dr. Clarke told him, "and no two teachers have exactly the same approach. There isn't *one right way* to conduct a conference.

"After all," Dr. Clarke said, "a writing conference is just a conversation with a writer. If you heard one of your neighbors talking to a friend and you admired how much at ease he seemed to be as a conversationalist, you still wouldn't think you had to adopt his mannerisms and conversational style, would you?"

"So what do I do if every writing conference is different?" Rob asked his mentor. "How do I know what to do in each case?"

Rob's question was a good one—one you may be asking yourself.

First, remember the principles explained in the previous chapters. Before you can conference writers, you must be a writer yourself, and your classroom must be the type of place where writers can flourish, where "writing talk" permeates the atmosphere.

In that type of writing climate, what are you trying to accomplish when you conference a writer?

The answer is simple: The goal of every conference is to inspire the writer by showing interest in what he or she has to say. Don Graves' (1983, p. 66) classic book on the writing classroom, *Writing: Students and Teachers at Work*, calls this "receiving" the work of the author.

Graves used *receive* to mean that the writing teacher listens to and honors the words of the writer. Children need to discuss their work in a helpful, caring exchange. Young writers are very vulnerable when writing. They need to be shown respect and tenderness through supportive conferencing.

Lucy Calkins (1994) wrote about how the guru of all American writing coaches, Donald Murray, received her writing:

> I will never forget when I was working with Don Murray on my own writing, how it felt when he casually made comments such as, 'Writers like you ...' or 'When you send this out ....' I held these phrases close to my heart, repeating them over and over. I remember even more how it felt to have Murray listening to my ideas and to my teaching, as they lived on my page. (p. 17)

Some students graduate from high school without ever being heard. They cannot recall a single incident in their entire educational careers when they wrote something in class and a teacher read it for meaning. Typically, when a teacher read one of their pieces, the teacher was reading to evaluate—to point out weaknesses, give instruction, offer advice.

When you conference a student, you are the first audience for that piece of writing. Many teachers intentionally leave their pens at their desks when they conduct conferences, just so they won't be tempted to make corrections on a student's paper.

Before we can focus on writing improvement, we must let writers know they have been heard. We must focus on meaning by reacting to the message, not the medium in which it has been delivered.

Only when students know that we are more interested in what they have to say than how they have said it, when they know that we approach them as a reader and not a critic, will they feel free to take risks in their writing. Remember, children develop language through interaction. Just as they learn to talk by talking to someone who responds, typically a parent, they learn to write by writing to someone who responds. That's you.*

Rob found this a liberating idea. He did not have to be like his experienced colleague down the hall. Instead, he began to circulate among his students during writing workshop as an experienced writer "talking shop" with younger writers. Rob's students came to look forward to his passing by their desk, offering a cheery, "How's it going?" or "This piece coming together okay for you?"

Sometimes they would respond with a smile and an "I think you'll like this one." Sometimes they would ask a question. Sometimes they would shrug and sigh, and Rob would kneel down and ask, "You want to read some of it to me?"

But whether the conference was fifteen seconds or five minutes, Rob had one primary goal: to inspire the writer by his interest in what that writer had to say.

As Rob developed more confidence in his ability to conference writers, he saw more and more evidence that his genuine interest in meaning and the time he devoted to being a good audience was paying off through his actions, he was encouraging his student writers to focus on meaning.

---

*The social constructivist perspective on learning, articulated principally by Russian psycholinguist Lev Vygotsky, offers some interesting insights here. Vygotsky said that learning proceeds from the *inter*psychological plane (between individuals) to an *intra*psychological plane (inside the individual)—with the help of a knowledgeable member of the culture, like a teacher. Vygotsky held that language mediates experience, transforming mental functions (see Lev Vygotsky, *Mind in Society: The Development of Higher Psychological Processes*. Cambridge, MA: Harvard University Press, 1978, and Elizabeth Petrick Steward, *Beginning Writers in the Zone of Proximal Development*. Hillsdale, NJ: Lawrence Erlbaum Associates, 1995). That means that when you talk about the processes and products of writing with a student, you are helping that student literally to *learn to think* about the act of writing in a way that would have never been possible unless the young writer could have "talked out" his or her writing process.

Something to think about

Are you focusing on meaning when you conference writers? Are you really listening to what writers have written? Are you reacting as a teacher or as a reader?

If you were to meet a novelist at a book signing, you wouldn't say, "I enjoyed your book, but I think the opening was a little long-winded and you really didn't help me visualize the setting properly." You would tell the author what you liked and you would talk about the plot, perhaps asking questions if there was something you didn't understand.

And certainly you wouldn't leave the book-signing guilty that you hadn't said anything that would make the author a better writer. That wasn't your goal—you just wanted to talk about the book with the author.

Try adopting that same strategy this week with your student writers.

References

Calkins, L. (1994). *The art of teaching writing* (2nd ed.). Portsmouth, NH: Heinemann.

Graves, D. (1983). *Writing: Teachers and children at work.* Portsmouth, NH: Heinemann.

CHAPTER 6

Learning From the Therapists

None of Sandi's faculty colleagues knew that she was seeing a counselor. Battling depression over problems in her marriage, Sandi decided to see a therapist before the situation got out of hand.

After only a few sessions, Sandi began to get perspective on her problems, and after two months she discontinued her counseling appointments, feeling that she would now be able to continue working through her problems on her own.

In her very first appointment with her therapist, Sandi noticed that he was using some of the very same techniques she used in her conferences with her fourth-grade writers. And though she didn't realize it at the time, the writing conference movement owes much to the writings and techniques of psychological therapists and counselors. Any writing coach could benefit from reading Carl Rogers' (1951) classic *Client-Centered Therapy*, where Rogers explains the goal of the therapist as releasing the client's capacity to deal constructively with life—thereby giving that person power to resume control and move forward.

As Sandi's therapist listened to her describe the problems in her marriage and some of the other stresses in her life, he saw his job as helping her to think through and reevaluate her problems. He wanted to put her back in control so she could move forward with a clearer sense of direction. He also wanted to prepare Sandi for her future by helping her to deal effectively with the present.

Although the therapist could have given Sandi a list of what he thought she was doing wrong and how she could change, he didn't. Instead, he served as a *facilitator* for her growth, not an authority figure whose job it was to give her the answers. He offered help by helping her to help herself.

That was exactly the role Sandi herself adopted as she conferenced her fourth-grade writers day after day in writing workshop. Like the therapist, the writing coach helps students:

- "think through" their writing problems by creating an atmosphere of acceptance and trust, by listening to the writers as they talk through their ideas, and by asking the types of questions that help writers focus on potential solutions
- see the big picture—how to take techniques used by trade book authors or ideas discussed in minilessons and apply them to their writing
- see the coach as a collaborator who helps them brainstorm ideas and think more creatively, not as the "answer person" who merely offers solutions in conferences.

This approach to conferencing requires more than just knowing about the writing process and about conferencing techniques. It requires that the writing coach be committed to a philosophy—that writing is more learned than taught and that writers must see the value of writing and want to appropriate its benefits before they become teachable.

Carl Rogers (1951) said the same was true for the therapist. He said nondirective counseling began not with counseling techniques, but with the philosophy of the counselor. As you read through Rogers' questions for a therapist, ask them of yourself as a writing teacher:

> How do we look upon others? Do we see each person as having worth and dignity in his own right? If we do hold this point of view at the verbal level, to what extent is it operationally evident at the behavioral level? Do we tend to treat individuals as persons of worth, or do we subtly devaluate them by our attitudes and behavior? Is our philosophy one in which respect for the individual is uppermost? Do we respect his capacity and his right to self-direction, or do we basically believe that his life would be best guided by us? To what extent do we have a need and desire to dominate others? Are we willing for the individual to select and choose his own values, or are our actions guided by the conviction (usually unspoken) that he would be happiest if he permitted us to select for him his values and standards and goals? (p. 20)

This approach is not the invention of 20th-century psychotherapy. In fact, you could learn much about writing conferencing by reading the dialogues of Socrates. Note how he used the technique:

Socrates calls to Meno's little slave boy, a child without education.

"Tell me, boy, do you know that a figure like this is a
square?"

"I do."

"And do you know that a square figure has these four
sides equal?"

"Certainly."

Socrates continues to ask the boy questions, draw-
ing diagrams as he does so.

"Do you observe, Meno, that I am not teaching the
boy anything, but only asking him questions? Well, what
do you say to that? I didn't just tell him that! I just asked
questions. He must have known it already. It was in him!
All that knowledge." (Plato, trans. 1984, pp. 164–171)

The writing conference draws on an age-old technique—engaging
the learner in conversation to help him or her think through the problem
at hand. Socrates could have saved a lot of time by explaining the concept
of the square to the boy, but that would have demonstrated Socrates' mas-
tery of the concept, not the boy's.

Some teachers claim they do not have time to engage students in
conferences. So where do they find time to explain the same concept over
and over again, to pile illustration on top of illustration, to continue to
correct the same errors?

Like the therapist does with the client, the writing coach helps the
writer to think through a problem, to examine possible solutions, and to
decide on a course of action and determine to implement it.

Something to think about

Do you dispense *Writer's Welfare*? That is, do you spend lots of
time telling writers what they should do to improve their writing,
rather than helping them to think through the process themselves?

Some teachers occasionally carry a micro-cassette recorder
with them during conferencing to record what goes on, then play
the tape back during their drives to and from work. What they
often find is that they talk too much, listen too little, and ask too
few questions to stimulate writers to think.

References

Allen, R. E. (trans.) (1984). *The dialogues of Plato, Vol. 1*. New Haven: Yale
  University Press.
Rogers, C. (1951). *Client-centered therapy: Its current practice, implica-
  tions, and theory*. Boston: Houghton Mifflin.

CHAPTER 7

Creating Confident Writers: The Effective Use of Praise

Jack put down his pencil and looked up from his page at his class. He wished he had more time for the piece he was working on about rock climbing, his weekend hobby and a real topic of interest for his fifth graders.

As Jack looked around at his writers, Patricio caught his eye. Patricio knew the routine well—when Jack put down his pencil about 10 minutes into writing workshop, it meant his teacher was about to begin circulating around the room to talk with students about their works in process.

Patricio's hand was up before Jack had time to stand. He motioned for his teacher to come to his desk.

"You're excited about something," Jack whispered to Patricio. "What's up?"

"I finally finished my poem about basketball," Patricio said. "Can I read it to you?"

"I can't wait to hear it," Jack said as he knelt down on one knee and rested his elbows on Patricio's desk. Jack's body language was that of an eager and interested listener.

"I got my idea from *The Football That Won*" (Sampson, 1996), Patricio said, alluding to his favorite book, which used the pattern in *This Is the House That Jack Built* to tell the story of a Dallas Cowboys Super Bowl victory.

Patricio began:

"This is the center who dunked the ball that won the playoffs in overtime.

"This is the guard who passed to the center who
dunked the ball that won the playoffs in overtime.
"This is the...."

Patricio went on to read his poem, occasionally looking up at Jack, as the rapt attention of his teacher gave him added confidence. That confidence was reflected in Patricio's voice, which got louder as he read. By the time he finished, he had the attention of several students near him who had stopped their own writing to listen.

Finished, Patricio lowered his paper and looked at Jack, awaiting his response.

"Patricio, thanks for letting me be your first audience for that poem," Jack said. "You know what a basketball fan I am, and your poem helped me to visualize the game as you told about it through poetry.

"You have a lot of really concrete images there, Patricio. You wrote about a behind-the-back pass and a fast break; you even mentioned the sweat on the coach's forehead when his team went behind by one point with only 10 seconds left. That's good writing.

"I'll bet the author, Michael Sampson, would like to read this poem, because you were able to take his pattern from *The Football That Won* and extend it to another sport.

"So what do you plan to do now with the piece?"

Jack's comments to Patricio showed that he understood the value of praise in a writing conference and that he knew how to make praise work as a motivator for writers.

Jack *could* have said: "Great piece, Patricio. I really liked it. You're getting better and better as a writer."

And while that sounds good, praise that praises the writer, not the writing, can backfire for young writers.

In a writing conference, we are trying to produce self-reliance, self-direction, and inner motivation. Children can become dependent on such praise for their self-worth as a writer. Praise-dependent young writers must show everything to the teacher for their daily affirmation.

Look again at what Jack *could* have said. It clearly focuses on qualities of the writer, not the writing. There's nothing there for the writer to hang on to. He is told that he is a good writer, but not why.

Now reread what Jack actually did say. He told Patricio *why* his poem was good. He specifically mentioned Patricio's use of concrete images. He made the connection between Patricio's poem and a well-known trade book and complimented him on using that as a writing model and extending it.

Learning to praise young writers is a key to making conferences work. A great beginning point for learning how to conference is to receive the writer's work (see Chapter 5), to be a great first audience. But after we have listened intently and demonstrated our interest in what the writer has to say, where do we go from there? Many writing coaches look for something positive to praise in the student's work.

And what if there is little to praise? Generally there is *something*— a nice phrase, a good image, an appropriate choice of words, or even a unique topic nobody else has written on before. Writing teacher Ralph Fletcher (1993) comments on how good teachers can find something to praise even in mediocre pieces of writing:

> Like a good music teacher, the writing teacher endures the bad melodies and shaky rhythms, stays patient, and picks out moments when the writing works well. It might be but a sentence: 'The roller coaster went upside down and stopped like a bat hanging from a tree.' It might be a single phrase. Even in a 'bad' piece of writing, the mentor reaches into the chaos, finds a place where the writing works, pulls it from the wreckage, names it, and makes the writer aware of this emerging skill with words. Careful praise of this kind can fuel a writer for a long time. (p. 14)

Praise is most effective when it describes the writing, not the writer. Praise works when it tells writers specifically what they did well. This motivates writers to keep on writing, to take chances, and to work even harder on the areas where they have already demonstrated their success.

Something to think about

Here's how you can begin this week to implement constructive praise as a strategy when you conference writers.

- Go back for a quick reread of Chapter 4, Learning to Talk Writing. You will be most effective in praising your students' writing when you are comfortable talking about writing techniques.

- As practice, take several writing portfolios home, representing a wide range of students' abilities. Find a piece in each and read it. Then pretend you were conferencing that student. How could you share effective praise based on what you just read?

References

Fletcher, R. (1993). *What a writer needs.* Portsmouth, NH: Heinemann.
Sampson, M. (1996). *The football that won.* New York: Henry Holt.

CHAPTER 8

How to Question Without Interrogating: Using Questions to Focus on Writing Issues

Renee returned to her fourth-grade classroom full of enthusiasm for conferencing after the weekend seminar she attended. On her desk was a 3 × 5 notecard covered front and back with questions the speaker had suggested for use during conference time.

But after several days, she was disappointed. She felt she had given conferencing a fair shot, but it just hadn't gone over with her kids.

"I've asked every question on my list," she confided to a colleague during lunch, "but it just doesn't feel comfortable and I don't think the students are getting anything out of our conference time."

Renee had made the mistake lots of teachers make when they first begin conferencing writers. She wasn't having a conversation about writing—she was playing "20 Questions" with the writer. Her conferences were more like a police interrogation than helpful talk about writing.

Questions are crucial to the writing conference, but conferencing is much more than questioning a writer. In fact, there's danger in the lists of questions you so often find in books on writing teaching: We feel obligated to ask them.

Questions should be considered in the context of what we're trying to achieve when we sit down to talk with a writer of any age. Muriel Harris (1986) stated it succinctly:

> Talking with students as they write or prepare to write
> indicates that we view writing as a process of discovery in

which we can help the writer learn how to shape a piece
as it is taking form. (p. 5)

Some texts on writing conferencing miss the entire point of asking questions. It's not to lead the writer where we want him or her to go or to motivate revision—although those may well be the by-products of a conference. Instead, we want to let the writer know that he or she has been heard, to act as a first audience for a piece, and to both empower and teach the writer through praise. Beyond that, we want to help students "talk out" problems they are having or verbalize their plans for the piece.

One of the things that makes writing difficult is moving from the pictures in our heads, sometimes the abstractions in our heads, to paper. How many times have you heard an adult writer say, "I know what I want to say—I just can't get it down on paper." If adults have that problem, perhaps young writers experience it even more acutely as they try to move from thoughts in their minds to words on their page.

What conferencing does is to add an intermediate stage. We help writers talk about their writing topics. Writers get a chance to tell us about conversations they had, they describe actions and their feelings about those actions, and they see how dialogue or description would be appropriate for their pieces. Now they're not writing down what they're thinking; they're writing down what they just heard themselves say.

A newspaper journalist entered my office for a writing conference on a story he was working on. It was the type of story most journalists hate—it was about economic trends, and it was full of statistics and boring economic forecasts.

Although we were friends, he had not one word of greeting as he entered my office for the writing conference. He walked in, tossed his story on my desk, and said: "Here. Take it. It's awful."

"Oh?" I said as I reached out to turn the story upside down on my desk so he wouldn't have to look at what he obviously considered a bad piece of journalism. "Why's that?"

"It's boring. I wouldn't read it myself if I were one of our readers."

"Why not?" I asked.

He went on to tell me what he considered to be wrong with the story. I asked him what he thought it needed. He told me, and then I asked him how he could get the material he said the story needed to make it more reader-friendly.

After he told me several things he thought he could do to improve his piece, I reached out to turn the story over to read it.

"Mind if I take a few minutes and look it over now?" I asked.

"Never mind," he said, reaching for his story in my hands. "I know what I need to do. Thanks."

I shook my head as he walked out of the office with his story. We had just concluded a 20-minute writing conference on a story this journalist had been working on for a week. He came in frustrated and left full of plans for changes he hoped to make.

And I never read even one word of the story!

The journalist was frustrated over his inability to take a complicated story and make it interesting and relevant for his readers. He had tried and failed to move from the conceptual level in his mind to the printed word. But when he heard himself talking about his options, it all clicked. He left to write down what he just heard himself say.

That's the function of a conference—to help the writer think like a writer.

Questions can be used during a conference to clarify the student's problems and concerns and to motivate planning that can later be written down.

Here's what questions can do:

- **Questions can open the conference.**   Many teachers begin a conference with "How's it going?" or "What's this draft about?"

- **Questions can help writers clarify problems.**   Here's a conversation overheard in fourth grade:

Ms. Quinn:	How's your football piece, Kevin?
Kevin:	Not too good.
Ms. Quinn:	Not good? What's the matter?
Kevin:	You know I said I was going to write about how our team pulled together and won three straight games after our best running back got kicked off the team?
Ms. Quinn:	Right...
Kevin:	But I don't know whether to start with Rodney getting kicked off the team or us getting chosen to play in the championship tournament.
Ms. Quinn:	Which would make the most interesting lead?
Kevin:	Well, I could start with Coach telling us we had been selected for the tournament. We all thought we had played our last game and we were just coming to turn in our pads. Boy, were we surprised! But if I do that, how to I get back to the first of the season when Rodney was suspended?
Ms. Quinn:	Just asking that question shows you're really maturing as a writer, Kevin. But let's take first things first. Why not go ahead and write about that scene where you found out about

the tournament? When you finish, let me know and I'll show you some examples of how writers use flashbacks in their writing. [Ms. Quinn also makes a mental note at this point that some of her students would probably benefit from a couple of minilessons on writing with flashbacks. She knows she can use Kevin's story as an example of how flashbacks can be worked into writing.]

- **Questions help writers deal with process issues.**   Typical questions include: What do you plan to do next with this piece? What will you do about illustrations? Is this one of the pieces you might like to take on to publication? You said it needed some more description of the spooky old house—where do you think that description should go to be most effective?

- **Questions give writers insight into their own writing development.**   It's important to help students think through their own processes so they can see how they are growing. It also helps them distill principles they can use again when they write. Some questions: Where did you come up with this idea? That description was especially vivid—how did you make it seem so real? How did you choose that lead? Do you think your ending is as strong as your beginning? What part do you like best? What part do you like least?

Questions are one of the tools the writing coach uses to help students think through their development as writers as well as particular problems on a specific piece. But asking questions must never become an end in itself. Lucy Calkins (1994) wrote that the purpose of asking questions "is to understand the writer." She continued:

> The questions will come, of course, but they are not the goal. They are the by-products of our efforts to understand our students. I am stressing this point not to devalue the questions we ask but to empower them. When our questions grow out of our emerging understanding of the writer, they are alive and fresh and powerful. When the same questions grow only out of a chapter on good questions to ask in writing conferences, they quickly become canned and mechanical. (p. 225)

Some teachers are concerned that their conferences might become predictable. They're right, and that's okay. Think, for instance, about your telephone conversations with your best friend. How many times have you said, "What's up?" or "You don't say?" or "Why's that?" Face it: You're predictable in conversations. But those questions are asked in different contexts. And when your friend calls up, she really *wants* you to say, "What's up?" because she wants to tell you about her day.

When your writers see that you too are a writer willing to share your processes and products with them, they will eagerly want to talk with you about their works in process. As you become more comfortable with conferencing, you'll probably notice that you use four or five questions over and over. But listen to two of your young writers peer conferencing together, and you'll hear them ask the exact same questions of each other.

Something to think about

Have you been asking questions more as an interrogator and less as a coach? Susan Sowers (1988) put it this way:

> We sometimes forget that a good conference is a workmanlike conversation about writing in progress—not an interrogation. We rehearse provocative questions when we ought to listen to the writer or to the writing. We are poised, ready to engineer a breakthrough in revision with the right question.
>
> Our vigilance is commendable. But faith in the power of the right question is misplaced. There are no magic questions. (p. 130)

References

Calkins, L. (1994). *The art of teaching writing* (2nd ed.). Portsmouth, NH: Heinemann.

Harris, M. (1986). *Teaching one-to-one: The writing conference.* Urbana, IL: NCTE.

Sowers, S. (1988). "Reflect, expand, select: Three responses in the writing conference." In Newkirk & Atwell (Eds.), *Understanding writing* (2nd ed.) (pp. 130–141). Portsmouth, NH: Heinemann.

CHAPTER 9

Students Helping Students: Teaching Young Writers to Conference Each Other

How can you tell that writing conferencing is really working in your classroom? One of the best ways is when you notice that you're not doing all the conferencing: The students are spontaneously coaching each other in peer conferences.

Donald Graves (1994) wrote about his less-than-successful attempt to initiate peer conferencing in his seventh-grade classroom:

> I simply said, 'Okay, I want you to exchange papers and respond to each other's work. Listen carefully, take the paper back, and return to your writing.' What I got was a massive blood-letting: first wails, then silence. My students went into shock. Their responses were not helpful. At the time, I couldn't understand why peer-response didn't work. In retrospect, I realize that they responded to each other as I responded to them—with nit-picking criticism. (p. 108)

Graves admits that the initial failure of his experiment in peer conferencing was the result of the weakness of his approach to writing teaching. But even teachers who use a writing coach approach must make special preparations for peer conferencing.

How do you know if your class is ready to be introduced to peer conferencing? Ask yourself these questions:

- Is writing a normal part of your classroom routine? Do your students write every day?

- Are your students accustomed to a routine of conferencing? Do you regularly conduct writing conferences with students?
- Do you present minilessons that explain writing techniques that relate to real-life writing problems students are having with their pieces? (Real-life "writing talk" in minilessons helps students become familiar with the how-to's of writing and helps them to relate their comments in peer conferences to topics already discussed in class.)
- Do you write with your students and give them an opportunity to "conference you" on your pieces by asking you questions and making suggestions that motivate revision and editing in your writing?

If you answered yes to all of these questions, your class is ready for peer conferencing. And if you couldn't answer yes, forget peer conferencing for the time being. Deal first with those other issues, and then introduce peer conferencing.

So if you believe your class is ready, how can you teach peer conferencing and get your young writers ready to conference each other?

- **Try author's chair.**   Author's chair, a popular strategy in process classrooms, is a place where children share books they have written or a trade book they enjoyed. After the student reads the book, classmates respond by telling what they liked: "I liked the part where you got lost in the mall and you were afraid you would never see your mom again." "I liked the way your story ended. It surprised me!"

  Then classmates ask questions about the text: "Why did you choose that topic?" "Did your dog really get run over and die?" "I thought the dinosaurs would fight at the end. Why didn't you have them fight?" If the student reads a trade book, he or she will speculate on the answers the author might have provided.

  Author's chair is an effective way to introduce the concept of peer conference in a roundabout way, because it features an interaction among students about a text. Young writers become accustomed to asking and answering questions, and they participate in a basic format that they can then transfer to peer conferences: Tell what you liked and ask questions about anything you did not understand.

- **Explain and demonstrate peer conferencing.**   Peer conferencing doesn't come naturally. It has to be first demonstrated, then taught. Your conferencing with students is the best model you have for peer conferencing. In fact, when both you and your students come to see teacher-student conferences as a normal part of the classroom environment, peer conferencing will automatically start—even if you never teach it or encourage it or use the words "peer conference." Students will begin to ask some of the same questions you do and conference each other. But you can help the process along by teaching how to do peer conferences in a minilesson. Then you can role-play a typical peer conference with a student. Lucy Calkins (1983), writing in *Lessons From a Child*, passed along a peer conference format taught by a New Hampshire fourth-grade teacher to her class:

1. Writers would begin by explaining where they were in the writing process, and what help they needed. For example, a child might say, 'I'm on my third draft and I want to know if you can picture it,' or 'I have six titles and I can't decide which is best.'
2. Usually, but not always, the writer would then read the piece—or the pertinent sections of the piece—out loud.
3. The writer would call on listeners. Usually listeners would begin by retelling what they'd heard, 'I learned that ...' they'd say, or 'Your piece began ...' Sometimes they'd begin by responding to or appreciating the contents of the piece.
4. Questions or suggestions would then be offered, not about everything, but about the concern raised by the writer. Sometimes other things would come up as well, but not always. (p. 126)

Peer conferencing, like writing, is a developmental process where learning is ongoing. Keep coming back to the topic in minilessons to deal with issues raised in peer conferences you will overhear.

- **Structure peer conferences, especially at first.**   Even though you have demonstrated and explained peer conferences, it will help to provide an outline for conferences. Barry Lane (1993, p. 109), a Vermont writing teacher, suggests the following outline for conferences:

    √ I like:
    √ I wonder:
    √ Questions:
    √ Plan for action:

Lane suggests that the conference partners are responsible for the first three parts of the outline: They tell the writer what they like about the piece, tell what they wonder about it, and then they ask questions. In response, the writer devises and shares a plan of action for any revisions following the conference.

Eventually, peer conferences will become real conversations among writers. But students are not accustomed to talking about writing in process, so to jump-start the peer conferences, provide a conference format at first and spend plenty of time teaching about and role-playing peer conferences. The time you invest in peer conferencing will pay off by involving your whole class in the conferencing process.

Something to think about

Steven Zemelman and Harvey Daniels (1988) share insight about involving peers in the writing process. They point out that peer strategies don't usually work well the first time they are tried in the classroom:

> [Peer conferencing] is probably the single most abandoned element of the process paradigm; many teachers and even a few researchers will tell you that they tried peer editing, and it doesn't work. The basic reason it is so hard to implement is that in our schools, students aren't often taught or encouraged to work cooperatively or to give respectful, insightful, constructive criticism. This is peculiar, since almost all of the work of real adult life is done by groups of people—offices, departments, staffs, teams, partnerships, crews—who must work collaboratively and exchange feedback if high-quality work is to be accomplished. (p. 191)

With Zemelman and Daniels' critique in mind, formulate your plans for introducing peer conferencing in your classroom. Look back through this chapter to see if your classroom environment seems conducive to the introduction of peer conferencing.

References

Calkins, L. (1983). *Lessons from a child*. Portsmouth, NH: Heinemann.
Graves, D. (1994). *A fresh look at writing*. Portsmouth, NH: Heinemann.
Lane, B. (1993). *After the end*. Portsmouth, NH: Heinemann.
Zemelman, S., & Daniels, H. (1988). *A community of writers: Teaching writing in the junior and senior high school*. Portsmouth, NH: Heinemann.

CHAPTER 10

Building Editing Skills in Conference

In their zeal to separate writing from editing, some writing teachers have gone too far in deemphasizing editing.

The process writing idea brought the perspective of real-world writing to the classroom. Before the process philosophy began to make an impact, many teachers approached writing merely as a product, not a series of processes that resulted in a product. These teachers didn't understand writing the way they did, say, baking a cake. No cook would combine flour and water, mix, and then taste and evaluate. Anyone who bakes knows that a variety of ingredients must be added over a period of time in the right proportions. Then comes mixing, then baking.

Writing works the same way. The process movement showed us that writers must experiment with ideas on paper, gradually watching them take shape through trial and error. Conferencing writers in process helps them to "cook" their ideas and make sense for the reader of the images and information in their heads.

Remember when you were in elementary school yourself, when teachers typically evaluated the "cake" before it was done? Our teachers told us what kind of cake to bake and how long it should stay in the oven. Frequently, all they cared about was the frosting on our cake and how it looked on the plate. They never tasted the words or experienced the images. They were editors at heart, forced to teach writing.

But if the teachers we remember did not understand how to teach writing, did they at least teach editing well? After all, that's where they spent most of their class time and their grading time.

The answer is clear: No, they didn't.

Think back to your elementary and secondary school years. Chances are, you wrote, and your teacher edited. The edited pieces were then returned, dripping in red, with admonitions to study the teacher's editing marks and avoid those errors the next time you wrote.

So did you? Of course not.

You wrote again, and you made the same mistakes, followed by the same red marks, followed by the same admonitions, voiced in ever-more-exasperated tones as the year progressed.

Why was your teacher frustrated? Because she continued to demonstrate her editing expertise without giving *you* a chance to develop yours. The problem was probably compounded by the fact that you were writing on a topic you hadn't selected for an audience of one, the teacher, whose only function was to grade what you submitted. The editing motivation just wasn't there.

Then came the process writing movement in the 1980s. We heard that writing and editing are two different functions and that, just as cooks shouldn't frost the cake until it has been baked, writers shouldn't edit until their piece is finished. And pieces that aren't destined for publication or presentation to an audience don't need to be edited at all. Why frost the cake and display it on a crystal plate if no one's going to eat it?

The process writing movement has properly deemphasized editing, but we must be careful to view editing the same way professional writers do—as a service to our readers. Journalist and writing coach Roy Peter Clark (1987) says the key to effective editing instruction is approaching grammar, usage, and mechanics as *tools*, not *rules*.

> I learned to punctuate when I stopped asking 'What's the rule here?' and began asking 'How can I use this comma to make my meaning clear?' The difference is profound. Emphasis on the rule inhibits the writer; emphasis on the tool has the writer reaching to his workbench for something that will help him. (p. 137)

Editing conferences are as valuable as writing conferences, and for the same reason. Both editing and writing conferences put the responsibility back on students for evaluating and making changes in what they have written. Teachers who edit student copy demonstrate their own editing expertise, but they don't develop the ability of the student writer to edit. Editing conferences help students "think through" the editing process for themselves.

Here are some ideas for initiating editing conferences in your classroom:

- Put aside one day a week for editing conferences. Unlike writing conferences, where you circulate through the room talking with writers in process, these conferences work best when students sign up to meet with you. You might arrange these conferences where you can sit at a table across from the student. You'll help avoid distractions if the student has his or her back to the classroom—and that will also put you where you can see what's going on while you're conducting the editing conference.

- Students should bring about three pieces to the conference (you can adjust that number to whatever works in your classroom). This will hold down the number of conferences because students will work at different paces in finishing the number of pieces you want them to bring to the conference.

  Your set of questions might be:

  "Of these three pieces, which do you like best? Why? Is that the piece you want to take on to publication? Why do you like this piece best? What did you do here that you didn't do as well in the other two pieces?"

  To answer these questions, students must think back through their writing process and make some value judgments. This helps them to identify their strengths and weaknesses as writers.

- Your next question might be something like this: "So what do you need to do to this piece to get it ready for publication?" That leads you into editing, and it emphasizes the role of editing in preparing a piece for readers.

  Many teachers use editing checklists appropriate for their grade level. In first grade, the student might leave the editing conference with a checklist that directs him or her to edit for capital letters and periods and spelling, for instance. The higher the grade, the more items on the list. Your editing checklist might include instructions to get a classmate to edit the piece before it comes back to you. (Some teachers also require peer conferencing for content before a student can sign up for an editing conference.)

  When the student has edited the piece and received editing input from a classmate, he or she can sign up for another editing conference to review the progress on the piece. You might use this second conference to give one-on-one instruction on a concept the student is having trouble with. If you see words still spelled wrong, you might put a light pencil mark next to lines that have misspellings, with instructions to the student to check words in those lines. Editing conferences will give you great ideas for minilessons; you'll be able to "scratch where it itches" and deal with the editing concepts students need the most.

- You must decide individually when to stop the editing process for each student. Some students will be able to find every error. But your objective is that each student develops his or her editing ability, learning something new on every piece.

  It's best to respond only to selected types of errors, focusing on the particular types of errors you have reviewed in minilessons. That means you may leave some errors unmarked. This bothers some teachers, until they look again at the big picture: that their function is not so much to improve the *writing* as to improve the *writer*. When you are satisfied that learning and growth have occurred, you can declare a piece finished.

- The next step will probably be publication of some sort. You can explain to students how major publication houses and mass circulation media work—that writers have an opportunity to self-edit, with various copyeditors and ultimately an editor-in-chief having the final say. In your classroom publishing house, you are that editor-in-chief.

Are students discouraged when the teacher corrects mechanical errors? Not when the teacher has explained that your classroom model works the same as the world of professional publications, and not when student writers can see that you are merely editing for mechanics, not taking over ownership of their pieces.

Something to think about

You will save lots of time in editing conferences if you work from an editing checklist. The checklist should include appropriate grammar, spelling, and punctuation items with which your writers are familiar. On the back of that checklist, you might include copyediting marks, so your writers can become accustomed to editing the same way professional writers do. If you want students to meet with a peer for content conferencing before they meet with you for an editing conference or to let peers have an opportunity to help with the editing, put that on your checklist, too. Ask colleagues for samples of their editing checklists. Many books on the writing process also include such lists.

References

Clark, R. P. (1987). *Free to write.* Portsmouth, NH: Heinemann.

CHAPTER 11

Conferencing to Encourage Revision

Revision literally means *to look again,* to rethink, to view what you wrote in light of what you wanted to write. It's definitely a higher-order writing competency, an ability that must be developed in writers after they attain fluency—that is, after they feel comfortable with the writing process.

Revision begins with thinking about what you have written. Sound familiar? The goal of the writing conference is to get students to think about what they have written.

Writing teacher Marge Frank (1995) notes that **revision** is driven by **response** to writing:

> Without feedback about the strengths and needs of the
> writing, the author has no real substance to take along to
> the task of revising the piece. (p. 36)

Young writers need that substance—ideas about writers' options. They also need the motivation to revise and instruction in the how-to's of revision. The writing conference can provide all three.

In the same way you create a climate for writing (see Chapter 14 for ideas on how to create a classroom climate conducive to writing), you must create a climate for revision in your classroom. Here's how you create that revision-friendly atmosphere:

- Model revision in your own writing. Let your students conference you on some of your writing, pieces that you do in writing workshop with them. Ask what questions they have about your piece. Ask if there is information you could include that would make the piece more interesting to readers. Make some of the revisions they suggest and let them compare your original piece to the revised writing. Before you teach revision in a minilesson, let them see by your demonstration that revision is an integral part of the writing process.

- Model revision in the writing you do together as a class. When you write a class book together, be sure to go back through it and look for opportunities to revise with a view toward making it more reader-friendly.

- Teach revision in minilessons. After you have modeled revision, you can move on to teaching the techniques of revision. Teaching the techniques of revision just takes the teaching of good writing techniques one step further.

For instance, you might have already taught some minilessons on how to use dialogue and how to punctuate correctly. Now you can show a piece that you have written that quotes all the characters indirectly through paraphrase, instead of through direct quotes. Or you can make some changes in dialogue the students are familiar with. You might try a paraphrase like this, of Bill Martin's (1985) *Ghost-Eye Tree*:

> The boy's sister asked what was the matter.
>
> He said his hat had slipped off.
>
> She accused him of being afraid, but he said he wasn't.
> He then told her he was going to get his hat.

Then show the kids Bill Martin's original version, told in dialogue:

> "What's the matter now?" my sister asked.
>
> "My hat," I said. "It slipped off."
>
> "You're afraid, that's what!" my sister said.
>
> "I am not," I said. "I'm getting my hat." (Martin, 1985)

Young writers immediately see that the author's version has more life and more interest for readers because of the use of real dialogue. Show them in a minilesson how they can convert indirect quotes into direct quotes in their writing—that's a prime example of revision.

- Provide regular times to write every day. When kids write regularly, they stay oriented to the piece they are working on, and they don't lose touch with their intentions. This makes revision easier.

- Help young writers understand various types of revision. In-process revision is practiced by all writers. It's when writers realize that a stronger verb will give life to a sentence or a more specific noun will give readers a visual image. As writers come to realize this—from seeing you do it in your own writing and in the writing you do together as a class—they will be more likely to cross out and make changes as they write. The more mature the writer, the more frequent those in-process revisions come. The other type of revision is a true re-visioning of the entire piece, as writers take time to put themselves in the place of the reader and evaluate organization and clarity. Writers in the intermediate grades who have much experience in a process-oriented writing environment can begin to implement these types of revisions.

After you have created a climate for revision, you can use writing conferences to help students think like writers when it comes to revision.

Gary, a fourth-grade teacher in northern California, understands that writing conferences can focus a young writer's attention on information readers need and details that will make the piece more interesting.

"How's your football piece coming, Ryan?" Gary asked one of his young writers. The day before, Ryan had told him excitedly about a story he was writing based on a game his Youth League team had played earlier that week.

"I think I'm almost finished," Ryan said. "You want to hear the part about where I catch the pass for the touchdown? It's the best part."

"Read on," Gary said, bending down to eye level with Ryan and settling in to a listening pose his young writers knew guaranteed them his undivided attention. Ryan read the section to his teacher:

> The Bearcats were behind 7-0 and the coach knew the game was on the line. He called a pass play and the quarterback threw it to Ryan, who ran 40 yards for a touchdown. The game ended in a tie, but at least the Bearcats didn't lose.

"That sounds like an exciting play," Gary said. "What kind of play was it?"

"It was a halfback fake," Ryan said, his voice getting louder as he talked. "The quarterback faked it to the halfback and the halfback acted like he had the ball. Then he rolled out and threw it to me. I was playing wide receiver. All the defense thought it was a running play. We faked them all out. When he threw it to me, none of the Tigers was anyplace close. I ran in for the TD without anybody even touching me."

"That's a great story," Gary said. "When you told me the story just then, it was even more exciting than when you read it to me. That's because you gave me a lot of information that helped me see that pass play in my mind. Telling me the quarterback faked to the halfback and then threw to you gave me a mental picture of the play. Would you like to include a couple of extra sentences to give your readers that information?"

"Sure," said Ryan. "And that would make a great illustration, too."

"Exactly," Gary said. "Now where in your piece would that additional information go?"

As Marge Frank noted, the response drove the revision. Gary and other teachers like him who use conferencing as a strategy with their writers have learned that conferencing motivates revision because it helps young writers to rethink their writing as they talk with their teacher-coach.

Something to think about

Young writers need to see revision in perspective. Not all pieces should be revised. In fact, not all pieces need to be finished. Demonstrating revision in your pieces and presenting occasional minilessons on revision will keep the revision process in the minds of your students.

Remember these ideas about revision:

- The reason to revise is to help the reader, so unless you have a publication program and an opportunity to share writing publicly, there is really no reason to revise.
- Differentiate between revision and copyediting for grammar, spelling, punctuation, and word usage.
- If you teach primaries, remember not to expect too much revision. It's just not developmentally appropriate for most first and second graders. But even with primaries, we can demonstrate revision in our own writing, though we typically won't see it in the writing of most of our students.

References

Frank, M. (1995). *If you're trying to teach kids how to write...you've gotta have this book*. Nashville, TN: Incentive.

Martin, B., Jr., & Archambault, J. (1985). *The ghost-eye tree*. New York: Holt.

CHAPTER 12

Teaching Young Writers to Conference Themselves

Conferencing works because writer-to-writer conversations focus the attention of young writers on what they are trying to say. They encourage students to "think like writers" in the following ways:

- Teachers react initially to the content of the writer's communication—not the format or the writer's effectiveness in saying it. This helps students focus on the real reason to write: communication.

- Teachers praise writers when appropriate and remind them of what they know and the progress they are making. Thus this helps them to feel confident of their developing abilities.

- Teachers encourage writers to take risks and to try new things without fear of failure.

But as valuable as conferencing is, the goal is not that every student should have to participate in a writing conference to produce an effective piece. Rather, we want to ask the kinds of questions writers ask themselves and talk about the types of concerns that writers must consider when they write—with the ultimate goal that students will internalize the principles of the conference.

We want students to *conference themselves.*

One way we achieve this is through predictability in our conferences.

Students in Mary Beth's fifth-grade class know that they will have a chance for a short one-on-one with their teacher at least every other day. After Mary Beth conducts a 10-minute minilesson on some aspect of writing, the class begins to write. They know that their teacher will write with them for about 10 minutes, and then for about 20 minutes she will circulate among them conducting short conferences ranging from one to three or four minutes.

Mary Beth's students know that she will typically approach them and ask "What's happening with your piece?" or "How's this one coming?" If everything is going well, she might ask them what they're writing about or ask if they would like to read several sentences for her. She might also ask what part they are working on now or what they plan to do next. They know that if they have questions or problems, she will help them to think them through or refer them to a book that contains the answer or perhaps another student who successfully wrestled with the same problem.

Mary Beth doesn't solve their writers' problems; she helps her students to think through the problems or locate the answers to them. She knows that the quickest way to deal with one of her fifth graders' questions is to answer it. But that creates a dependency on the teacher and casts her in the role of the "answer person." Instead, she wants her students to learn how to think through their writing issues on their own.

Another way Mary Beth helps students learn to conference themselves is to let them conference each other. Peer conferences help her students internalize the way conferencing works because they have to actively think about what their conference partner has written (see Chapter 9). They have to find what works in the writing and come up with questions about things they didn't understand. This helps them to learn to read and listen like writers, a skill they can then use on their own writing.

Each year, after her students become accustomed to writing conferences, Mary Beth introduces peer conferencing. When she feels peer conferencing is working effectively in her room, she introduces the self-conference.

Writers self-conference themselves when they take off their writer's hat and read like readers, looking for places where the writing works and where it doesn't. Mary Beth introduces the self-conference in a minilesson where she explains how it works.

She tells her fifth graders that they can do a self-conference any time they want to by pulling out a self-conference guide that she has photocopied and distributed for them to add to their writer's notebooks. Here is the guide:

> Read your piece through again. Now ask yourself these questions:
>
> - How do I feel about it?
> - How else could I have done this?
> - Have I tried anything I never tried before?

- What's the strongest part of the piece?
- What's the weakest part?
- What will I do next?

After Mary Beth taught about self-conferences in a minilesson and modeled several self-conferences by talking herself through the questions on pieces she has written during workshop time, she encourages her students to try it. Sometimes, during her conference time, she will ask a student to pull out the self-conference guide. She typically tells students that she will check in with them later in the workshop to see what insights or questions they came up with during their self-conference time. Her one-on-one with them will then revolve around insights or questions they came up with during self-conference time.

The self-conference obviously works best with intermediate-level writers, but even primaries can be encouraged to read their pieces to themselves to try to identify parts a reader would be most interested in.

Something to think about

Self-conferences encourage students to think about their writing metalinguistically and metacognitively. That is, they are thinking about how they use language on paper and about how they think. They are thinking about their own writing processes—and that is the very essence of the process-oriented classroom.

Students typically don't begin to understand how self-conferences work until they see them modeled. Begin with something you wrote and "think out loud" on a self-conference. Then write something in the style and voice of a typical student writer in your classroom and play that writer as you act out his or her self-conference, again thinking out loud. If a student shares an insight with you that he or she came to in a self-conference, ask that student to consider sharing it with the group during share time.

CHAPTER 13

Finding Time to Conference

It's the most frequently asked question about conferencing in the classroom: *How do I find the time to fit conferencing into my already overcrowded day?*

There's no one right way to structure conferences, so successful teachers will have different answers to that question. Fitting conferencing into writing workshop time becomes much easier, however, for teachers who aren't laboring under the myths about conferencing.

Here are some of those myths and the rebuttals to them:

- *Myth No. 1: The way to conference is to sit down with a writer and read the entire piece and then talk about it.* Let's look at the two types of conferences:

    √ In-process conferences (some teachers call them content conferences), where you talk briefly with the writer while the piece is being written. These conferences are short—typically lasting a minute or so—and are initiated by the teacher. During these conferences you talk with students about where they are in the writing process, answer questions, and sometimes listen to leads or paragraphs or short sections of a work in process. Only rarely—and mostly with primaries—would you read or have the student read to you an entire piece during an in-process conference.

    √ Editing or publication conferences, where you help the writer begin the journey toward eventual publication by focusing on editing or revision. These conferences take longer and are initiated by the student writer, who signs up for an editing conference when he or she has completed several pieces. You will read more of a piece during an editing conference because you are helping the student focus on editing for eventual publication.

- *Myth No. 2: Teachers need to talk with every writer every day.* That's impossible! Holding a brief in-process conference with every writer once a week is a more reasonable goal.

- *Myth No. 3: Teachers read student writing in every conference.* Sometimes just the act of reading the student's writing puts you in the role of the "expert" or the evaluator. It is expected that you will assess the quality of a piece or prescribe a fix.

  But writing coaches are looking for the long-term benefits of working with writers, not just their products. So sometimes you will just talk about the progress on the piece at hand; sometimes you will ask a writer what he or she is working on and give a word or two of encouragement; sometimes you will acknowledge a question or problem and suggest a resource—either another writer who has faced that problem or a classroom reference book or a trade book in which the author faced the same writing dilemma.

  You might spend 20 minutes on in-process conferences with your fifth-grade writers and never read one word they have written.

- *Myth No. 4: Students should be conferenced on every piece they write.*   Now that's a recipe for early teacher burnout! Instead, every student should know that the teacher circulates among writers holding short conferences during writing workshop, and there's a chance he or she will get a conference-visit from the teacher any day. Students should know that the teacher is available to answer questions during that conference time, but the answer is likely to be a reference to a person or another learning source. And students should know that when they complete several pieces, they can sign up for an editing conference where their writing will have the teacher's undivided attention.

- *Myth No. 5: Conferencing is so time-consuming because you need to deal with all the problems and errors you see when you read a piece of student writing.*   Keep in mind that the first priority is that the students know they have been heard, that teacher-coaches are genuinely interested in their information or their stories.

  Beyond that, writing coaches generally look for the progress students are making so they can encourage writers by reminding them of what they're learning. ("You must have really been paying attention during my minilesson this morning on descriptive writing! Look at how you've captured the look of this character. I can get a mental picture of her when I read.")

Coaches then look for teachable moments—opportunities to extend what students know. ("I like the way you have used dialogue in this piece. Letting me hear an actual conversation between the girl and her mother makes your story seem more authentic and involves the reader much more. Do you remember our minilesson a few weeks ago on how to punctuate quotations? You already have quotation marks around all the quoted statements. Now all you need to do is work on getting your commas, periods, question marks, and exclamation points in the right places. Why not look up the pages on quotations in our language arts book and check out where those marks go? You might also want to compare what your language arts book says with the book you're reading right now. Isn't it Beverly Cleary's *Ribsy*? You'll find lots of examples of what your textbook tells you about punctuating quotations.")

The Peace Corps used to point out in its advertisements that its mission in developing countries was a long-term one. Give a man a fish, the ads said, and he will eat for a day. Teach him to fish and he will eat for a lifetime. Handing out fish takes less time than teaching fishing. But in the long term, teaching fishing was actually a better use of time.

Teachers face the same dilemma in the classroom every day. When you become accustomed to working with short conferences, you'll find that they don't take up as much time as you might have feared. And the time we spend conferencing is our best investment in helping kids think like writers.

Something to think about

Another myth looms as large in some teachers' minds as those discussed above. They think they shouldn't begin conferencing students until they feel they have a handle on the conferencing process and can do it well.

But what if we applied the same principle to writing: Don't write until you're a good writer. We can never become a good writer, of course, until we write.

And you can never get good at conferencing student writers until you try it. The more you do it, the better you'll get. But while you're learning, you're demonstrating your willingness to talk writing, you're serving as a first audience to works in progress, you're praising writers for what they're doing well, and you're getting an insight into your writers that will pay dividends in your minilessons.

Learning to conference is a process, just like learning to write. And as with writing, you learn by doing.

CHAPTER 14

No Palm Trees in Cincinnati: Establishing an Environment for Teaching Writing

I did a double-take as I drove down a street in a suburb of Cincinnati. Outside a large supermarket designed on a jungle theme was a row of palm trees lining the parking lot. I did a U-turn back to the store for a closer look. Sure enough, they were real. But how do you grow palm trees in Ohio? I went in to ask that question of a manager.

Her answer: "You don't."

"Some years we lose lots of them to the cold," she explained. "And when we do, we just bring in new ones."

The bottom line: If you see a row of palm trees in the Midwest, you know someone is fooling with Mother Nature.

In horticulture, as in the writing classroom, climate is everything. If you plant palm trees in a cold climate, you can implement all the right growing strategies. You can have a palm tree professional take care of them. You can give them all the nutrients a healthy palm could ever need. But they won't grow; the climate isn't right.

Many teachers have tried transplanting strategies and methods into their writing classroom. And the strategies were effective ones—suggested by the likes of Donald Graves or Donald Murray or Lucy Calkins or Nancie Atwell, or perhaps by another classroom teacher at a workshop. Teachers took these new strategies—like writing conferencing, for example—back to their classrooms, confident that they would be successful.

Problem was, they didn't work. And, when that happened, the strategies became another entry on that teacher's great-sounding-process-oriented-ideas-that-didn't-work-for-me list.

Why didn't those strategies work? Why does writing conferencing work for one teacher and not for another?

It could be for the same reason palm trees will grow in Miami but not in Cincinnati: climate.

There is a climate in which process-oriented strategies like the writing conference will flourish, and a climate in which they will die. And it has nothing to do with the teacher's sincerity or knowledge about conferencing. There are some classroom climates where writing conferencing fits perfectly, where it's consistent with the tone and mood and direction of the class. In these classrooms, writing conferences are a sure-fire winner.

So what are the characteristics of this classroom climate?

- **Teachers model the writing process:** The starting point for building a writing program is that the teacher is a writer who shares his or her processes and products with the class (see Chapter 3). In this classroom:

    √ Teachers usually write along with students during writing workshop. When students look up from their writing, they see their teacher engaged in the same process they are experiencing.

    √ Teachers model the writing process for their students. During brainstorming sessions, they share topics they are considering writing on that day. In this way they model the process of topic selection. They share their drafts with their students and let their class see their markouts and changes and awkward attempts at lead-writing.

    √ Teachers publish for their classes, taking some of their writing and illustrating it with photos or art and adding the final product to the classroom library.

    √ Students see the teacher as a writer because they are able to observe the teacher at every stage of the writing process.

- **Teachers immerse the class in great books and beautiful language:** Teachers surround their students with the best literature they can find. Enter this classroom and you're likely to find the teacher reading to students. They may be reading a picture book or a chapter book or an article from that morning's newspaper or a few paragraphs from a novel the teacher is currently enjoying.

    These teachers realize that to get beautiful language out of student writers, you have to expose them to great prose stylists and poets. These teachers don't read just so that students can analyze or answer comprehension questions or fill out worksheets or complete a project. These teachers read because they want to share the books they love, so that students can fall in love with those same books. And much of what students fall in love with eventually makes its way into their writing. Mark Twain realized this a century ago when he wrote:

> Whenever we read a sentence and like it, we unconsciously store it away in our model-chamber; and it goes with a myriad of its fellows to the building, brick by brick, of the eventual edifice which we call our style. (Bainton, 1890)

Immersing children in a world of good books affects more than their writing style, however. It also helps them to think like writers, to see more possibilities for writing topics. Mem Fox (1993) said that students who are not exposed to good books live in a "literary desert" where good writing ideas cannot bloom:

> We need to water the desert so the writing will bloom. By watering the desert I mean providing children with the most wonderful literature available: the classics, the new, the beautiful, the revolting, the hysterical, the puzzling, the amazing, the riveting. We need to fill their storehouses with events, characters, styles, emotions, places, and themes that will help them to grow, not wither, thirsty in the desert of illiteracy. (p. 67)

- *Teachers invite students to spend more time with some books and authors.*   Teachers find authentic ways to invite students to get to know some of the books, poems, and authors in which students have been immersed. Students are invited into a deeper experience—through author studies, choral reading, or dramatization of a book, comparison of two similar works, art activities, or writing book ads or book reviews. Students are immersed in lots of literature, but they are encouraged to have a deeper experience of some of those books and poems.

- *Young writers examine techniques used by writers they are reading.*   On some of the pieces they study, teachers take time to point out the composing techniques of the writers. How does this work? A classroom favorite might be Bill Martin Jr.'s (1986) *Barn Dance*. Teachers might want to invite students to know the work better through a choral reading. Many classes dramatize the book, but the teacher may also want to use the book when the class is looking at lead-writing. Perhaps in a minilesson the teacher will show different ways that authors begin their stories. The teacher might even want to rewrite the beginning of the book like this:

> Once there was a boy. He lived on a farm. One night he wasn't sleepy. He heard something in the barn.

And then, contrast Bill Martin's lead:

> Full moon shinin', shinin' big an' bright,
>
> Pushin' back the shadows, holdin' back the night.
>
> Not a thing stirrin', quiet as could be,
>
> Just the whisper of the leaves on the cottonwood tree. (Martin, 1986)

When you study descriptive writing, for example, show lots of examples of description from the books that are already so much a part of the classroom experience. Students know the books and the authors—now let them in on the author's techniques, the things that writers do to draw readers in and keep them interested.

- *Teachers make writing an everyday experience.* Children must experience writing themselves through writing workshop response journals, and writing across the curriculum. No one—child or adult— ever gets comfortable with writing until it becomes part of a regular routine.

  If you can drive a car with a standard transmission, you no doubt remember your first few times behind the wheel. You were conscious of every move. You watched the speedometer because you had been told about how fast to go in each gear before you shifted. You were very conscious of putting your foot on the clutch, pushing all the way in, checking the speedometer, then shifting. But now? You would probably find it hard to explain the process because it has become second nature to you. You do it without consciously thinking. You have become a *fluent* driver. Kids become fluent writers the same way we become fluent drivers: practice. Regular writing is an integral part of a good writing climate.

- *Teachers present the skills and conventions of writing in context.* Process-oriented teachers talk a lot about teaching skills in context. What does that mean? It means that we begin by writing ourselves. In that context, we immerse children in good books. In that context, we invite them to experience some of those books and writers more deeply. In that context, we explore the composing techniques of some of those writers. In that context, we provide daily opportunities to write. And in the context of *all* of those activities, we teach the skills students need to enhance their writing. Those skills include grammar, spelling, punctuation, and word usage. When they are taught in the context of a reading-writing classroom, these skills or conventions come to be seen as valuable tools for writers.

- *Teachers help young writers find an audience.*   We cannot provide a climate that encourages writing unless we give students an opportunity to share their work with others, so they can see the effects of their words. That means we give students a chance to share their writing in author's chair, (Harste, Short, & Burke, 1988, pp. 219–220) to display their writing, or to publish their work in book form.

    In the context of all these activities, we employ strategies like the writing conference. And they work. In the classroom just described, the writing conference is a natural part of the classroom atmosphere because:

    √ students are already accustomed to "talking writing" when they discuss the composing techniques of authors;

    √ students write every day, so they feel more comfortable with the act of composition and less self-conscious about their writing;

    √ students see writing as such a normal part of classroom conversation that teachers can refer in conferences to writing techniques the young writers are already familiar with; and

    √ students trust the teacher because they see the teacher as a writer who is willing to take a chance alongside them.

When you transplant conferencing into a writer-friendly classroom climate, it is much more likely to take root and flourish as a popular and productive activity.

Something to think about

Take a few minutes to review each characteristic of the class-room climate that encourages writing. Be honest as you evaluate your classroom. Though you picked up this book to learn more about how to conference young writers, perhaps you see now that conferencing isn't really the issue, that you need to take care of other more basic issues before you introduce conferencing. Based on what you read in this chapter, what do you need to do to make your classroom climate conducive to growing writers?

References

Bainton, G. (Ed.). (1890). *The art of authorship: Literary reminiscences, methods of work, and advice to young beginners, personally contrib-uted by leading authors of the day.* New York: Appleton.

Fox, M. (1993). *Radical reflections.* San Diego, CA: Harcourt Brace.

Harste, J. C., Short, K. G., & Burke, C. (1988). *Creating classrooms for authors.* Portsmouth, NH: Heinemann.

Martin, B., Jr., & Archambault, J. (1986). *Barn dance.* New York: Holt.

EPILOGUE

So Now What?

You've finished the book. You now have insight into the nature and function of conferencing in the process-writing classroom. You understand more about different types of conferences and the part they play at each stage of the writing process. Perhaps you're already putting into practice the ideas you have picked up as you came to understand how conferencing works.

Remember several things as you begin to implement writing conferencing in your classroom:

- **There is no *one right way* to conduct a writing conference.** Conferencing styles differ according to the personality of the teacher and the nature of the class. Writing conferences are basically conversations between more mature writers and less mature writers about works in process.

    Let's say you are a veteran gardener. You don't know everything there is to know about gardening, but you have planted gardens for several years in your back yard. Your neighbor sees your garden and wants to start one of his own. You see him planting and you go next door. You chat with him about what he's doing. You don't take over his garden; instead, you just talk with him about his planting or fertilizing or watering. You compliment him on his successes. Since he knows you're a veteran gardener who wants to see his garden succeed too, he feels free to ask you questions as he works. You might take 30 seconds to answer a question on how far apart to plant seedlings, or you might spend a couple of minutes complimenting the brilliant color of his marigolds, or he might ask you to come next door and take his shears and show him how to prune his roses properly. You demonstrate, then he takes the shears and does it while you watch, then he is on his own.

If you can do it with gardening, you can do it with writing. It works the same way. And you can no more script a writing conference than you could script a month's worth of interactions with your neighbor about gardening.

- **Conferencing is a skill, and skills take time to develop.**   You can read a biography of Henry Ford and feel you have a really good understanding of the great auto maker's life. But you wouldn't read a book about driving and enter a NASCAR race. You practice on parking lots, then country roads, then neighborhood streets, gradually gaining confidence and skill before you attempt to drive on busy freeways.

  So why expect to master writing conferencing overnight? A popular board game advertises itself as taking "a minute to learn, a lifetime to master." That would also be an appropriate slogan for conferencing, so be patient with your initial attempts to initiate conferences in writer's workshop.

- **It may also take time for your students to feel comfortable with conferencing.**   You have probably been to a party—perhaps even hosted one—where the conversation was strained at first. People made awkward small-talk, and no one seemed conversationally comfortable. Perhaps some people even left the party early. But as the evening wore on, people loosened up and there was talk and laughter, and you had a hard time getting a word in because the conversation was flowing so freely. The people who left early gave up too soon. Don't you give up too soon: If students are not accustomed to "talking writing," it may take some time for them to loosen up and become comfortable conferencing to feel normal. But conferencing will begin to feel normal if you have the other elements of the writer-producing classroom atmosphere outlined in Chapter 14.

- **Teachers learn conferencing best when they practice on each other.**   Perhaps the best way to learn to conference is to get together with a few other teachers and form a writer's group. Meet once every two or three weeks to share something you have written since you last met—fiction or nonfiction, prose or poetry. The selection you choose to read or photocopy to hand out should be short, taking no more than a few minutes to share. After each participant has shared with the group, other group members conference that writer. Just follow the guidelines for conferencing in this book: Find something you liked, ask a question, discuss the author's writing process, make a suggestion.

Sometimes we are reluctant to put ourselves in that position of vulnerability by sharing our writing with our colleagues. But that's exactly what we're asking our students to do in writer's workshop. Participating in conferencing with your colleagues will help you identify with your young writers.

- **And most importantly, let students see you "in process" as a writer and give them opportunities to give you group feedback on your writing.**   You win your right to talk writer to writer with students in conference by demonstrating that you are a writer yourself, just like you win the right to talk with your neighbor about his garden when he sees that you have put time and effort into your own garden.

Final Thoughts

And what can you expect in your classroom as conferencing gradually becomes a part of your routine? You can expect your classroom to become a community of writers. You can expect students to take writing seriously because they will realize that its purpose is to communicate meaning with an audience. You can expect your students to mature as writers because they will have spent time discussing their own writing and gaining insight into their own composing processes. And you can expect to enjoy your interaction with your young authors more than ever before.

Using Anecdotal Records in Writing Conferences

by *Lois Davila*

When I conferenced my first graders, I used to tell my children it was important for me to "take some notes so I can remember what we talked about." I asked the children to help me by making sure that I "write something down" when we talked.

I made my notes on 3 × 5 cards and date-stamped them in the same way the children dated their pieces, and I filed them in shoe boxes almost daily. What a system, I thought! I was taking notes with the children's help and filing them with great efficiency.

But once they were filed, I did not find myself using them to inform future writing conferences or to evaluate the result of my minilessons and my day-to-day conferencing.

The "shoe box filing system" was too cumbersome for me to bring back and forth to school. So it didn't prove practical and teacher-friendly—important elements for affecting the quality of the instruction and learning taking place in our classroom.

The index cards did help me to develop the habit of taking anecdotal records and to learn how to notate key questions. But now I needed to learn to organize my notes to make them more useful.

I turned to professional books, journals, and conferences to seek out what others were doing and to share my questions and concerns with other writing teachers. I found that some teachers were using Post-it® notes, some were writing on the back of the child's piece, and some were making notes directly in the child's writing folder. My own experiences and the work of many other writing teachers led me to the beginnings of my current system. Even now, in my sixth year of record-keeping and assessment, the fine-tuning and adjustments continue.

In her book *And With a Light Touch,* Carol Avery (1993) suggested creating a weekly class list (kept on a clipboard) that helps to track the children you have conferenced (see figure 1). Raising your hand for attention is no longer a part of our writing workshop—hand-raising was a way children controlled where and to whom I would give attention.

Some children would raise their hand continuously and others very seldom. All children need to talk about their work. Using the class list on a clipboard, I can better track my attention to all children. The quietest, busiest children can otherwise easily be overlooked because they have *the look* of a writer hard at work. Often, their needs are similar to others who are more overt in displaying their needs.

In addition to moving about the room, I now make notes on strips of adhesive-backed address labels (1½ inches tall and 4 inches wide) that you can buy at any office supply store (see figure 2). I date-stamp each recorded conference and carry the strips of labels for several days on my clipboard together with the class list. This allows me to check back over progress during a six- to seven-day period when talking with the children. The notes are helpful in reminding both the children and me about specific ideas and suggestions made during the conferencing and provide a basis for evaluating what children do as a result of our conferencing together.

The adhesive labels transfer easily into a Class Workshop notebook. The notebook—I use a 3-inch looseleaf, with a divider for each child—for placing notes on each child. The labels collectively provide a continuum of what each child is doing and needs to do next as a writer.

I use the notebook, together with the child's cumulative writing folder, when I talk with parents about their child's growth in topic choice, use of conventions, spelling, phonics skills, choice of genre, and quality of response both to minilessons and to small-group and individual conferencing sessions.

At the bottom of the weekly class list is space for recording minilessons and possible ideas for upcoming lessons. Space is also provided to record high-frequency words (HFW) used by the children who need some attention, as well as words that are nearly conventional in their spelling. These words will be given attention and placed on our Word Wall to provide the needed support that will help the children gain control of these words both as readers and writers.

Inventories for the emergent and early writer and the fluent writer developed by Janine Batzle (1992) in her book *Portfolio Assessment and Evaluation* look at the child's writing process and product. They provide a framework to periodically summarize the gathered information and identify important next steps in both the teaching and learning for each child—and for our class as a whole—as we journey as a learner-centered classroom.

Writing Workshop – Daily/Weekly Conferring Records

Week of: **October 20-24ᵗʰ**

	Mon	Tues	Wed	Thurs	Fri	Comments
Alanna		✓	✓⑤			⑤ Counting Book / One Pumpkin
Andrew	✓	✓✓				
Brandon	✓				✓⑤	⑤ good start to counting book
Daylon		✓✓		✓		
Deirdre				✓⑤		⑤ proud – good voice
Dominick					✓	
Ethan	✓		✓			
Falon		✓	✓⑤			⑤ fluent, easily reread work, answered questions well
Ian		✓			✓	
Jessica	✓⑤			✓		⑤ quiet voice -- good story / Fall
Joseph	✓⑤				✓	⑤ beginning stage /extend!
Kayla		✓⑤		✓		⑤ retold story vs. text
Leighanne	✓			✓		
Lindsay	✓✓				✓	
Michael		✓✓			✓	
Michelle			✓⑤			⑤ confident, enjoyable!
Natalie		✓	✓			
Nicole	✓	✓⑤				⑤ conventional spellings "Me and my family"
Raymond			✓		✓⑤	⑤ TRYING HIS BEST!
Ryan			✓			
Samantha	AB	AB		✓⑤		⑤ Disney World journal
Thelma	✓				✓	
Vincent		✓✓	✓			
Zakariah			✓		✓⑤	⑤ good ideas, language!

Mini-lessons: <u>Concept of sentence -- using capital letters, punctuation, "1 finger space" between words. Use L/S knowledge</u>

HFW:
the to is and you (Spelling List)

✓ **conference**   ℗ **publishing**
✓✓ **check back**   ⑤ **shared in Author's Chair**

Figure 1   Sample Conferencing Form—Completed

Samantha--   SEP 17 1997
* more talk about trip to Disneyland
=> oral story- good print/text beginning

Kayla--   SEP 17 1997
* going to Aunt's house
* play w/ baby cousins
needs wait time and specific direction/support

Ethan-
- able to retell   SEP 17 1997
using the pix - good!
- comfortable, fluent, good detail in oral story

Ian--   SEP 17 1997
needs to reuse text
"I left some words out"
=> beginning self-monitoring

Daylan--   SEP 17 1997
rattlesnakes slithering in my garden
1 story/line; refocus before starting another story

Vincent   SEP 19 1997
"Me and my Dad were playing tennis..."
(just beginning)
=> lots of talk about Dad

Zakariah--   SEP 19 1997
"I saw a dragon and he was breathing fire at me" (no word boundaries but able to work indep w/s/s, message

Leighanne--   SEP 18 1997
"Me and Lindsay are in her pool"
=> wants to be right about her spelling

Lindsay--   SEP 18 1997
"I'm dancing in my dance class"
=> "Me bas on the stah" (dancing)(stage)

Vincent--   SEP 18 1997
"I was playing ball"
=> simple pix, capable w/ s/s
1 line -> needs to "grow a story"

Ethan -SEP 18 1997 speedy S D
What will happen when I get needed ABC strip for my hamster?
letter 'w' --uses all capitals
getting better at 1-1 some matching
"doesn't hear word boundaries as he speaks"
* stretched at "hamster" HMRT

Ryan--   SEP 18 1997
"I am riding on my skateboard"
=> needs encouragement and support for writing text

Raymond-   SEP 18 1997
"We're having a party.....
2 mice came in"
"msc" = mouse   (fast worker!)

Figure 2   Date Stamped Adhesive Labels

References

Avery, C. (1993). *And with a light touch: Learning about reading, writing, and teaching with first graders.* Portsmouth, NH: Heinemann.

Batzle, J. (1992). *Portfolio assessment and evaluation: Developing and using portfolios in the K–6 classroom.* Cypress, CA: Creative Teaching Press.

About the Authors

Tommy Thomason is a former professional journalist who now teaches in the news-editorial sequence of the Department of Journalism at Texas Christian University. He also brings the perspective of a professional writer into elementary school classrooms, where he conducts writing workshops with children every week. Dr. Thomason is also the author of *More Than a Writing Teacher: How to Become a Teacher Who Writes*, a book that shows teachers how to become more comfortable with their own writing.

Lois Davila, who wrote the appendix, teaches first grade in Long Island. She speaks to thousands of teachers throughout the United States each year in workshops and in-service meetings.

Gloria Houston, who wrote the foreword, is Author-in-Residence at Western Carolina University. She is best known for her historical fiction. Her books include *My Great Arizona, The Year of the Perfect Christmas Tree, Littlejim,* and *Mountain Valor.*

Brod Bagert, who wrote the introductory poem for the book, writes poetry for adults and poetry for children to perform. His children's poetry books include *Let Me Be the Boss, Elephant Games, Chicken Socks,* and *The Gooch Machine.*

Author Index

Subject Index